D1265843

FOOTBALL IN THE
ACC
(ATLANTIC COAST CONFERENCE)

rosen publishing's
rosen central®

New York

JEREMY HARROW

To Jess and Josh

Published in 2008 by The Rosen Publishing Group, Inc.
29 East 21st Street, New York, NY 10010

Library of Congress Cataloging-in-Publication Data

Harrow, Jeremy.
Football in the ACC (Atlantic Coast Conference) / Jeremy Harrow. — 1st ed.
    p. cm. — (Inside college football)
Includes bibliographical references and index.
ISBN-13: 978-1-4042-1918-2 (hardcover)
ISBN-10: 1-4042-1918-8 (hardcover)
1. Atlantic Coast Conference—History. 2. Football—United States—History. I. Title.
GV958.5.A75H37 2008
796.332'630973—dc22

                                                     2007008954

Manufactured in the United States of America

On the cover: (*Top*) The Florida State Seminoles' offensive line gears up for a game against their state rivals, the Florida Gators, in November 2006. (*Bottom*) The University of Miami Hurricanes line up against the North Carolina Tar Heels in October 2006.

CONTENTS

INTRODUCTION

College football is much more than a sport. It's pride shared among friends. It's bragging rights against rivals. It's a chance for old classmates to reunite in the fall. It's a welcome mat for new freshmen. It's an opportunity for distant family to gather together on a holiday weekend to watch a bowl game. It's a tradition that goes back to the nineteenth century. In fact, it's all of these things that make college football such an exciting event.

This might surprise you, but college football has been around longer than professional football. The sport first rose to prominence among universities on the East Coast. Princeton challenged Rutgers in the first game in 1869. At that time, American football was played more like soccer. It then began to change into a game that looked a lot like rugby. This was an important step. Rugby is

Clemson's Memorial Stadium is one of the biggest and loudest arenas in all of college football. It can seat more than 80,000 screaming fans. In the 1940s, a coach of a visiting team nicknamed it "Death Valley."

a very physical, bruising game that is popular in England and Australia. Unlike soccer-style European football, rugby players carry the ball in their hands. They also have to fight their way through the opposing team to get to the goal.

A man named Walter Camp eventually came along with his own ideas about football. He gave the game its unique identity in the early 1880s. The first thing Camp did was to reduce the number of players on the field. The early days of football were characterized more by chaos than athletic competition. There were as many as fifty players on the field at any given time. Camp limited each team to eleven players and devised a more orderly way of moving the ball to the goal. The new system had both teams lining up against each other in a scrimmage. The team with the ball had three chances

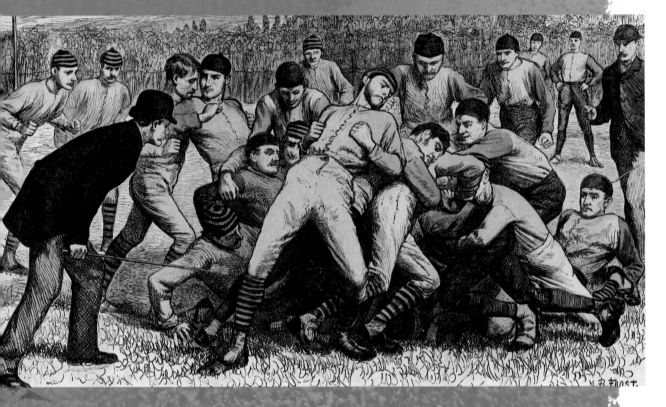

Above is an 1879 illustration of a Yale-Princeton football game in the pre–Walter Camp era. Helmets were not mandatory equipment in college football until 1939.

to get the ball across five yards. These chances were called downs. If they gained five yards, they would be given three more downs to advance toward the goal. This system was modified in 1912, when the rule was changed to require the gaining of ten yards within four downs.

Football fever began to spread to colleges everywhere after the new system was in place. These college games would become a great source of school pride. Mascots were created to rally the students for the games. Rivalries sprung up between nearby colleges. One region of the country where college football really took hold was in the South. A group of Southern colleges would form the first intercollegiate conference in 1894. A conference meant there would be games played between regular opponents who squared off against each other every year. Each team in the conference would vie for the best record and a chance to be conference champion. Today, there are sixty-six college sports conferences grouped in three divisions of the National Collegiate Athletic Association (NCAA; though the NCAA's Division I is split into two classes—Division I-A and Division I-AA).

While football is a game of tradition, it's also not afraid of change. It's a sport that has grown in leaps and bounds since its humble beginnings. As years went by, new equipment, new rules, and new ways to play the game were developed. Teams began competing professionally in 1895, and the National Football League was created in 1920. Games were first broadcast over the radio and then eventually were shown on television. More exposure led to more fans of the game. From just a small crowd of curious observers on a New Jersey field in 1869, the audience for college football has grown to millions of fans all over the country.

History of the Atlantic Coast Conference

The Atlantic Coast Conference (ACC) is one of only eleven conferences that play Division I-A football for the National Collegiate Athletic Association (NCAA). There are three divisions in the NCAA (with Division I divided into Division I-A and Division I-AA). Division I-A is the cream of the crop. These are the only teams that compete for the national championship. The best high school football players in the country will end up at Division I-A colleges. The best Division I-A football players will go on to the National Football League (NFL).

Of these eleven conferences, the ACC is one of the best. Its teams are consistently ranked in the Top 25 polls. They frequently play in bowl games, and there are national champions among them. Many of these schools are household names. For example, there's Miami, Duke, Florida State, and North Carolina. Or, perhaps you know them better as the Hurricanes, Blue Devils, Seminoles, and Tar Heels. Those are just a few of the great schools in the conference.

A Southern Tradition

College football has deep roots in the South. The first collegiate athletic conference in the country was started in 1894 between southern universities. This group became the southern Intercollegiate Athletic Association (SIAA). Eight schools in the ACC were once part of this historical association. In 1921, half the teams in the SIAA chose to break away from their parent organization. They became the Southern

A University of Alabama football player is pictured above. Alabama was a founding member of the Southern Intercollegiate Athletic Association.

Conference. All of the seven original members of the ACC played in the Southern Conference. The SIAA is no longer around, but the Southern Conference is still active as one of the oldest conferences in the NCAA.

Going Off on Their Own

On May 8, 1953, seven schools formed the Atlantic Coast Conference. The charter members were Clemson, Duke, Maryland, North Carolina,

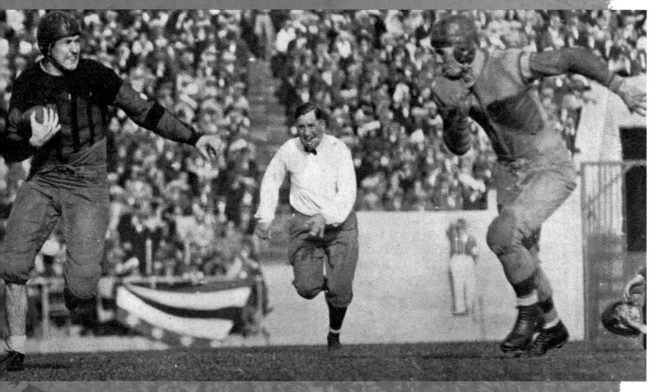

A University of Alabama runner gains yardage against a Washington Huskie defender as the referee sprints to keep up in the 1926 Rose Bowl. Alabama's win signaled the power of southern football and broke the stranglehold of college teams from the Northeast, Midwest, and West.

North Carolina State, South Carolina, and Wake Forest. The split from the Southern Conference was the result of several disagreements with the league.

One issue dealt with scheduling problems. There were seventeen teams in the Southern Conference before the teams that would form the ACC broke away. There was no way they could all play each other during the regular season because there weren't enough weeks in the schedule. Therefore, a mediocre team could end up with the best record if it didn't play the toughest teams and be declared the conference champion.

Seventeen teams also caused a lot of headaches for road games. Some of the colleges in the conference were far away from each other, and it was expensive to travel long distances. At that time, most of the schools didn't have large budgets for their athletic programs. A lot of them wanted to play more games against their rivals who were geographically closer.

More important, there was a big debate in the Southern Conference about the importance of championship bowl games. Not all teams in the conference thought bowls were such a good idea. College football was becoming more popular and attracting much larger crowds. Some games were now being televised nationwide, and a lot of money was now at stake for teams that reached bowl games. The competitive pressure to win was becoming greater. Colleges with a winning football team stood to make a lot of money

Short History of the NCAA

College football played an important role in the establishment of the National Collegiate Athletic Association (NCAA). It was a much rougher sport in the early twentieth century. There were far more serious injuries back then. Teams were not using the forward pass yet. One of the most notorious plays was called the flying wedge. Players would lock arms in a "V" formation to protect their teammate running the ball. The opposing team would throw themselves against the flying wedge to try to break it apart. It was like jumping in front of an avalanche. The action was violent and dangerous. In fact, eighteen players died in 1905.

President Theodore Roosevelt threatened to outlaw the sport. The colleges were ordered to make the game safer for their athletes. They formed the Intercollegiate Athletic Association of the United States (IAAUS) to enforce the new rules. The new national organization acted quickly to ban the flying wedge after another thirty-three players died. In 1910, the IAAUS changed its name to the NCAA.

(through television and merchandising revenue), boost alumni donations, and increase enrollment.

Some schools felt more emphasis was being placed on athletics than on education as a result of this new economic and competitive pressure. Finally, the Southern Conference voted to end its participation in bowl games. Clemson and Maryland opposed the ban and played in bowl games, anyway. The division between those who wanted bowls and those who opposed them was clear. It was for all these reasons that the seven schools created a new conference. Virginia joined the ACC at the end of 1953 to become the eighth member.

Coming and Going

The ACC has been a stable conference for most of its existence. South Carolina was the only school to ever quit the conference. It left in 1971 to improve its chances in postseason tournaments as an independent. Georgia Institute of Technology (Georgia Tech) came aboard in 1978. It was followed by Florida State in 1991. Until 2003, there were only nine teams in the conference.

Big Trouble with the Big East

By 2005, the ACC had expanded to twelve teams. This was a major expansion, and it was big news in college sports circles. The ACC aggressively pursued three of the strongest football programs in its conference rival, the Big East. The ACC invited Miami, Virginia Polytechnic Institute and State University (Virginia Tech), and Boston College to join its ranks. It would be a huge gain for the ACC if these teams switched conferences. However, it would also be a tremendous loss for the Big East. Although the Big East is known more for its basketball talent, it had created a football-only

Boston College officially joined the Atlantic Coast Conference on July 1, 2005. ACC commissioner John Swofford *(right)* presents Boston College athletic director Gene DeFilippo *(left)* with a plaque to commemorate the occasion.

conference in 1991. It was not going to let the ACC steal its best teams. After all, Miami was a five-time national champion. The Big East did everything it could to stop the expansion. It filed lawsuits and offered more money to the three schools to stay. It didn't matter. The temptation to join a better football conference was too great. Miami and Virginia Tech made the switch in 2004. Boston College completed the current ACC lineup in 2005.

Million$ of Reasons

There were some pretty big reasons for the ACC expansion. Division I-A conferences earn a lot of money for their schools by selling the

CURRENT ACC TEAMS AND THEIR ACCOMPLISHMENTS

SCHOOL	TEAM NAME	YEAR JOINED ACC	CONFERENCE CHAMPIONSHIPS	# OF BOWL APPEARANCES	BOWL W-L RECORD
Boston College	Eagles	2005	0	18	12–6
Clemson University	Tigers	1953	13	29	15–14
Duke University	Blue Devils	1953	7	8	3–5
Florida State University	Seminoles	1991	12	35	20–13–2
Georgia Tech	Yellow Jackets	1978	2	35	22–13
University of Maryland	Terrapins	1953	9	21	9–10–2
University of Miami	Hurricanes	2004	0	31	18–13
University of North Carolina	Tar Heels	1953	5	25	12–13
North Carolina State University	Wolfpack	1953	7	23	12–10–1
University of Virginia	Cavaliers	1953	2	16	7–9
Virginia Tech	Hokies	2004	1	20	7–13
Wake Forest University	Demon Deacons	1953	2	7	4–3

television rights to their games. A stronger conference meant that the ACC could get a better contract for its television rights. The addition of the three schools gave more muscle and value to the conference.

The conference convinced ABC/ESPN in 2004 to pay out around $38 million a year for seven years for the rights to broadcast ACC games. This nearly doubled its previous contract with the network. An additional television deal for syndication rights brought in several more millions dollars a year.

MOST RECENT BOWL APPEARANCE	# OF PLAYERS TO WIN HEISMAN	1ST-ROUND NFL DRAFT PICKS	# OF PLAYERS IN NFL HALL OF FAME	# OF PLAYERS/ COACHES IN NCAA HALL OF FAME
2006 Meineke Car Care Bowl: Boston College 25, Navy 24	1	14	2	8
2006 Music City Bowl: Kentucky 28, Clemson 20	0	21	0	5
1995 Hall of Fame Bowl: Wisconsin 34, Duke 20	0	6	3	11
2006 Emerald Bowl: Florida State 44, UCLA 27	2	33	1	5
2007 Gator Bowl: West Virginia 38, Georgia Tech 35	0	7	2	14
2006 Champs Sports Bowl: Maryland 24, Perdue 7	0	14	2	10
2006 MPC Computers Bowl: Miami 21, Nevada 20	2	58	4	5
2004 Continental Tire Bowl: Boston College 37, North Carolina 24	0	17	1	7
2005 Meineke Car Care Bowl: North Carolina State 14, South Florida 0	0	16	0	4
2005 Music City Bowl: Virginia 34, Minnesota 31	0	13	2	6
2006 Peach Bowl: Georgia 31, Virginia Tech 24	0	7	0	6
2007 Orange Bowl: Louisville 24, Wake Forest 13	0	3	1	0

A conference with twelve teams is allowed to have a conference championship game. A championship game gives the ACC more national exposure. More important, a conference title game is worth millions of more dollars on top of the ACC's two other television deals.

Two Divisions, One Conference

The ACC split the conference into two divisions in 2005. It needed two divisions to set up a conference championship game. Each division has six teams. The Atlantic Division is comprised of Boston College, Clemson, Florida State, Maryland, North Carolina State, and Wake Forest. The Coastal Division is made up of Duke, Georgia Tech, Miami, North Carolina, Virginia, and Virginia Tech. Florida State beat Virginia Tech, 27–22, in the first ACC conference championship game in December 2005.

All Winners

Five teams in the ACC have been declared the national champion of college football. The national champion usually is decided by the results of bowl games and different media polls. Miami has won five times. Georgia Tech has won four times. Florida State has won twice. Clemson has won once. Maryland won its only championship in 1953, the first year of the ACC. Don't feel sorry for the seven teams that haven't been national champions. Every team in the ACC has won a bowl game. Almost all of them have been conference champion as well. Virginia Tech won the conference in its first year as an ACC member. Only newcomers Miami and Boston College haven't won the ACC title . . . yet. The success of the teams in the ACC is why it is one of the best conferences in college football.

2 CHAPTER
Great Football Players of the ACC

The Atlantic Coast Conference has been producing great players for more than fifty years. They are the stars of the past, present, and future. Each has brought his unique talent and dazzling skills to the conference. Many have gone on to professional careers in the National Football League (NFL). There are two Heisman Trophy winners in this elite group. A few of them are already in the NFL Hall of Fame. Others are still making headlines on the field. Every one of them has earned the appreciation of the fans and the respect of their opponents.

Lawrence Taylor—North Carolina

The man known as "LT" was arguably the greatest linebacker to ever come out of the ACC. His Hall of Fame career in the NFL made

Lawrence Taylor (#98) was nicknamed "Godzilla" by his North Carolina coaches for his ferocious defense. North Carolina later retired his jersey number.

him a celebrity. In thirteen seasons playing professional football with the New York Giants, LT went to ten Pro Bowls, earned two Super Bowl rings, made 1,088 tackles and 132.5 quarterback sacks, and forced thirty-three fumbles. He was a defensive legend.

LT's success began with the Tar Heels. His greatest season with the University of North Carolina was in 1980. The team went 11–1 and easily captured the ACC championship. LT set a school record that year with sixteen sacks. His speed and strength made him the ACC player of the year and first team All-American. The New York Giants selected him with the second pick overall in the 1981 NFL draft.

Charlie Ward— Florida State

Florida State has a tradition of producing great quarterbacks. Charlie Ward set the standard for all of them. He was 22–2 as a starter. His 1993 season was the best ever for an ACC quarterback. He won every major award that year while taking the Seminoles to their first national championship. Ward was the first player from the ACC ever to win the Heisman Trophy. The Heisman is the top honor given to the best all-around player in the nation. He was such a gifted athlete that he was drafted as a basketball and baseball player. The only

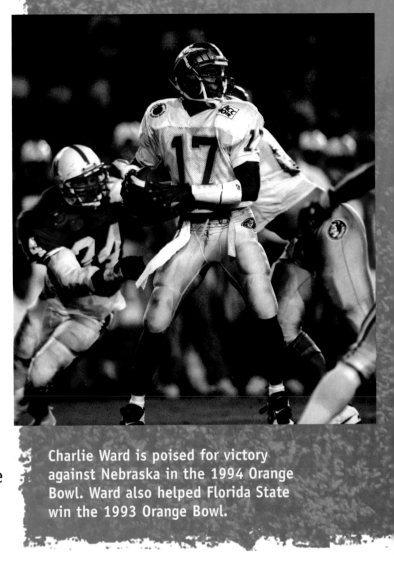

Charlie Ward is poised for victory against Nebraska in the 1994 Orange Bowl. Ward also helped Florida State win the 1993 Orange Bowl.

reason the NFL didn't draft him was because he was too small. Ward ended up playing point guard for the New York Knicks in the NBA. He was inducted into the College Football Hall of Fame in 2006.

Chris Weinke—Florida State

It was only fitting that the second Heisman Trophy winner ever from the ACC should be a Florida State quarterback. Charlie Ward left some big shoes to fill, but Chris Weinke had no problem filling them. He beat all the odds in 2000 as the oldest winner in Heisman Trophy history. Weinke was twenty-eight years old. He came to the Seminoles after a short career in professional baseball.

Weinke's record at Florida State was extraordinary. He was 32–3 as a starter over three seasons. In fact, he has the highest winning percentage in Florida State history. He led the team to three straight national title games. In 1999, he helped Florida State win its second national championship. It was the Seminole's first-ever undefeated season (12–0). Weinke threw for 4,167 yards in 2000 to

Brian's Song

Brian Piccolo was an All-American running back at Wake Forest. He was the ACC Player of the Year in 1964 after leading the nation in rushing and scoring. Despite his success, Piccolo was not picked in the National Football League draft. Most teams thought he was too small and slow to play professional football. The Chicago Bears signed him as a free agent instead.

Piccolo was determined to become a star, even though he was made a backup to Gale Sayers. The two teammates formed a special friendship. Piccolo was white and Sayers was black. They were the first interracial roommates in the NFL. Piccolo accepted his backup role until one season when Sayers was injured and could not play. Piccolo finally became a starter. He played well, but he also helped Sayers come back from his injury and reclaim his starting role.

Piccolo was still hoping to be a star when he was diagnosed with a rare form of cancer in 1969. He fought for his life and a chance to play again. He had surgery, chemotherapy, and radiation. Unfortunately, the cancer was too strong. Brian Piccolo died on June 16, 1970, at the age of twenty-six. His life story was featured in a 1971 television movie called *Brian's Song*, which was remade for broadcast in 2001.

lead the country. He is currently the backup quarterback for the Carolina Panthers in the NFL.

Philip Rivers—North Carolina State

Philip Rivers was a record-breaking quarterback for the Wolfpack from 2000 to 2003. He was NC State's starting quarterback for all four years of his college eligibility. The Wolfpack went to four straight bowls on the strength of his golden arm. They won three of them. He was the MVP for all four bowls and the Senior Bowl, too. Rivers started more games (fifty-one) than any

Philip Rivers completed thirty-seven passes for 475 yards and five touchdowns to crush Kansas, 56–26, in the 2003 Tangerine Bowl.

other quarterback in NCAA history. He had the best arm in the NCAA in 2003 with 348 completions, 34 touchdown passes, and 4,491 passing yards. His conference records are astonishing. Rivers is the all-time ACC leader in total offense (13,582), passing yardage (13,484), and touchdown passes (95). In 2006, he became the starting quarterback for the San Diego Chargers. Rivers led the team to the NFL playoffs with a 14–2 record.

Great Coaches of the ACC

Head coaches are the backbone of the college football system. It's their responsibility to recruit, train, and motivate their players. Once all the talent is gathered, each head coach has to turn this collection of players and strong personalities into a winning, unified, and smoothly functioning team. The head coaches set the tone for their teams. It's their vision that ends up on the field. They are the first to get all the credit and the first to get all the blame. The media will turn them into heroes or fools. The best head coaches stick around for years, while great players come and go. Some even end up coaching in the pros.

Bobby Bowden

Bobby Bowden is the first and last name of Florida State football. The Seminole coach has guided the team for more than thirty years.

He has more wins than any other coach in NCAA Division I-A history (366). Bowden's teams have been to thirty bowls and have won twenty of them. He is second only to Joe Paterno of Penn State in bowl appearances and wins. Florida State has won twelve conference titles in fourteen years (nine of them in a row between 1992 and 2000). It's enjoyed thirty straight winning seasons and two national championships (in 1993 and 1999). The Associated Press ranked Florida State in the top five for fourteen consecutive seasons (1987–2000).

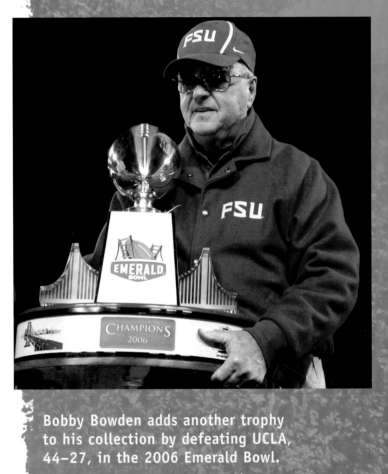

Bobby Bowden adds another trophy to his collection by defeating UCLA, 44–27, in the 2006 Emerald Bowl.

Bowden has coached two Heisman Trophy winners and enough future NFL players who could form a pro football "dream team."

Bowden is famous for his trick plays. His nickname is the "Riverboat Gambler" because he likes to take risky chances with a game on the line. His favorite trick plays are the "reverse" (when the quarterback hands the ball off to a running back or receiver who runs toward one side of the field, who in turn hands off to a receiver running in the opposite direction) and the "puntrooskie" (a variation on the fake punt in which the ball is hiked to an upback who hides it between his legs until a speedy ball carrier grabs it from him and runs upfield).

Ralph Friedgen

Ralph Friedgen had the perfect résumé for the Maryland coaching job. He played there as an offensive lineman. He began his coaching career there as a graduate assistant. He was also their offensive coordinator from 1982 to 1986. Friedgen had thirty years of experience as an assistant coach. As an offensive coordinator, he won a national championship with Georgia Tech and went to the Super Bowl with the San Diego Chargers.

Maryland hired Friedgen in 2000 to take over a weak football program. His first year was a smashing success. In fact, he was named the national Coach of the Year. He led Maryland to the 2001

John Heisman

John Heisman is the name behind the most famous award in college football, the Heisman Trophy, which is awarded annually to the best player in the country. Heisman coached for thirty-six years (1892–1927) and won 185 games. He is credited with creating the snap of the football from the center to the quarterback, and helping the forward pass become a standard play.

Heisman distinguished himself as a coach for two future members of the ACC. He coached at Clemson for four seasons from 1900 to 1903. The team went undefeated in his first season. In fact, they lost only three games in those four years. Heisman spent the best years of his career at Georgia Tech. He coached there for sixteen years and led the team to its first national championship in 1917. Georgia Tech earned 102 victories under Heisman and went undefeated for three straight seasons.

Heisman later became the athletic director for the Downtown Athletic Club (DAC) in New York, where he designed a system to annually select the best college football player in the country. The award was named after Heisman following his death in 1936.

ACC title and a trip to the Orange Bowl. They finished that season with a 10–2 record. The next two years led to more double-digit wins and two bowl victories. Friedgen was the first head coach in ACC history to reach ten or more wins in his first three seasons.

Frank Beamer

Frank Beamer has a long and happy history with Virginia Tech. He began coaching the Hokies in 1987. At that time, the football team was still an independent, belonging to no

Frank Beamer played defensive back for the Hokies as a student at Virginia Tech in the 1960s.

athletic conference. He guided its smooth transition into the Big East. The Hokies eventually won three Big East conference titles. In 1999, Beamer won eight national Coach of the Year awards. The Hokies finished second in the nation that year.

In 2004, Virginia Tech joined the ACC and won the conference title. Beamer was named the ACC Coach of the Year in 2004 and 2005. The Hokies have won ten or more games for three straight years (2004–2006). Equally impressive, Virginia Tech has had fourteen consecutive winning seasons (1993–2006). They also have appeared in fourteen consecutive bowl games. Frank Beamer is the mastermind of this football dynasty. He always gets the best out of

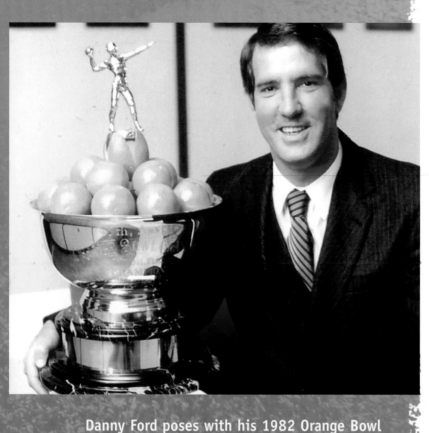

Danny Ford poses with his 1982 Orange Bowl trophy after winning the national championship against Nebraska.

his players. His 198 career wins is the third-highest total among active coaches.

Danny Ford

Danny Ford was only thirty years old when he became head coach at Clemson. He was the youngest coach in a conference full of experienced veterans. Ford took over the team right before an important bowl game. He rose to the challenge as the Tigers defeated Ohio State in the 1978 Gator Bowl.

Ford stayed at Clemson for eleven more years and amassed one of the best coaching records ever. The Tigers dominated the ACC for an entire decade. They were conference champions in 1981, 1982, 1986, 1987, and 1988. Their record for the decade was eighty-seven wins, twenty-five losses, and four ties. They had three straight seasons of ten wins or more. The Tigers won Clemson's first national championship in 1981. Ford took the nation's top coaching awards for that year. There were forty-one players on Ford's Clemson teams that went on to play in the National Football League.

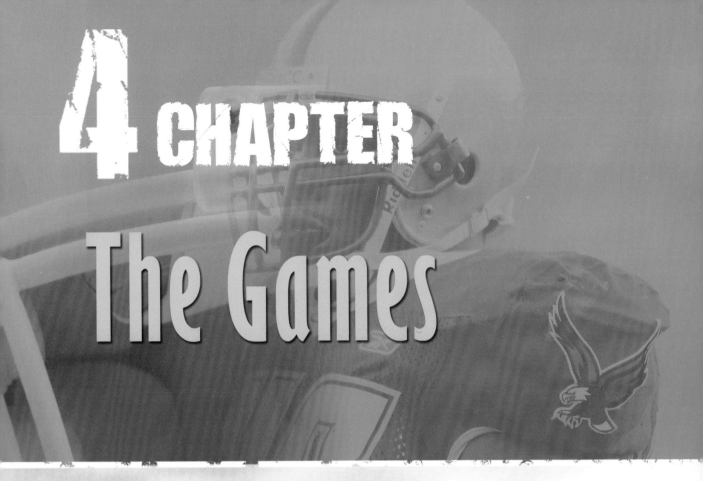

4 CHAPTER

The Games

The Atlantic Coast Conference is always full of exciting games. Its teams show up frequently on the Associated Press Top 25 poll, which ranks the nation's leading college football teams. They play a tough schedule against fellow ACC rivals and against the best teams from around the country. The conference's 2003 expansion to twelve teams made it possible for it to offer its fans even more excitement with a new conference championship game. Each school now has a shot at a division title as well as the conference championship.

Bowl Games

The first college football bowl game was played in 1902 in Pasadena, California. It was a postseason game meant to attract visitors to the Tournament of Roses festival. It was called the Rose Bowl, after the

Above is an illustration of the first Rose Bowl game in 1902. Michigan beat Stanford by a landslide, 49–0. The lack of excitement prompted the game's organizers to discontinue football in favor of Roman-style chariot races for the next fourteen years.

stadium that was built for it. Miami, Florida, witnessed the success of the Rose Bowl and was attracted to the idea of using a post-season football game to bring in tourists. It started the Orange Bowl in 1935.

Since then, bowl games have become a permanent fixture in college football. There are more than thirty of them. They usually are played from the last week of December through the first week of January. College football teams look forward to these games all season. A bowl appearance is a reward for a winning season. These games often determine a school's ranking on the final Associated Press Top 25 poll. The national championship is also decided in these games. ACC fans usually can count on seeing several of their schools competing in different bowls.

National Championship Games

The process of determining a national champion has changed a lot over the years. Division I-A football has never had a playoff system. Up until 1998, there was not even an official championship game. A team's ranking in various media polls and its performance in a major bowl game decided the national championship. The media polls would sometimes disagree and there would be two national champions named. Georgia Tech shared the 1990 national championship with Colorado. They couldn't play each other because they were playing in different bowls.

To help clarify this situation, the Bowl Championship Series (BCS) was created in 1998. The number one and number two teams would face off in one of four bowls. The four bowls took turns hosting the BCS championship. From 1998 to 2005, the Fiesta, Orange, Rose, and Sugar Bowls hosted the BCS national championship game. Florida State won their 1999 national crown at the Sugar Bowl. They beat Virginia Tech, 46–29. In 2006, the BCS added a national championship game that would be separate from the four bowls.

School Rivalries

School rivalries are one of the best things about college football. Colleges within the same conference play each other every year for the right to brag and gloat about being the best. Interconference games are the ones that energize the student body on every campus. They usually draw the biggest and loudest crowds of the season.

School rivalries go back decades and even longer. The Atlantic Coast Conference features a lot of rivalries that are older than the conference itself. These rivalries often have a lot to do with geography. Most of the original members of the ACC are either in the same state or neighboring states. In addition, the rivalries are not just within the conference. The ACC has a long tradition of school rivalries with the Southeastern Conference (SEC).

North Carolina vs. Virginia

This is called the "South's Oldest Rivalry." The two teams first played each other in 1892. The Virginia Cavaliers and the North Carolina Tar Heels have butted heads in 111 games since then. Virginia won the first contest by a score of 30–18. Virginia has the overall lead with fifty-four wins.

North Carolina vs. Duke

North Carolina has a lot of rivals within the ACC, but Duke is their archenemy. There is absolutely no love lost between these two teams. They face off every year in the "Battle of Tobacco Road." There are only a few miles separating the schools deep in the heart of tobacco-growing country. There is actually a trophy that goes to the winner of this annual duel. It's called the Victory Bell. North Carolina beat Duke in 2006 for their fifty-third win in the series.

Clemson vs. South Carolina

There are several reasons for this intense rivalry, which has endured for more than a hundred years. The biggest of these is state pride. South Carolina was a charter member of the ACC. They were also the only team ever to leave the conference. Now, they are a part of the

Two Clemson defenders close in on South Carolina QB Blake Mitchell in this 2006 contest between these state rivals. South Carolina ended a four-year losing streak against the Tigers with a 31–28 victory.

SEC. This rivalry began in 1896, and there was trouble from the start. The series was suspended from 1903 to 1908 because of a near-riot that broke out after the 1902 game. Cadets from Clemson were ready to march through South Carolina's campus to go to war. There was also a massive brawl during the 2004 game that led to suspensions of players on both teams. As of 2006, Clemson is in the overall lead with sixty-three victories.

Florida State vs. Florida

This is the real clash of the titans. It's much more than a state rivalry; this is about pure talent. These two teams are almost always at the

ACC Award Winners

Heisman Trophy
(College Football Player of the Year)

Year	Player	School
1984	Doug Flutie (QB)	Boston College
1986	Vinny Testaverde (QB)	Miami
1992	Gino Torretta (QB)	Miami
1993	Charlie Ward (QB)	Florida State
2000	Chris Weinke (QB)	Florida State

Butkus Award
(College Linebacker of the Year)

Year	Player	School
1987	Paul McGowan	Florida State
1992	Marvin Jones	Florida State
2000	Dan Morgan	Miami
2002	E. J. Henderson	Maryland

Bronko Nagurski Award
(College Defensive Player of the Year)

Year	Player	School
1994	Warren Sapp (DT)	Miami
1999	Corey Moore (DE)	Virginia Tech
2000	Dan Morgan (LB)	Miami

Lombardi Award
(College Lineman of the Year)

Year	Player	School
1974	Randy White (DT)	Maryland
1992	Marvin Jones (LB)	Florida State
1994	Warren Sapp (DT)	Miami
1999	Corey Moore (DE)	Virginia Tech
2000	Jamal Reynolds (DE)	Florida State
2001	Julius Peppers (DE)	North Carolina

Chuck Bednarik Award
(College Defensive Player of the Year)

Year	Player	School
2000	Dan Morgan (LB)	Miami
2001	Julius Peppers (DE)	North Carolina
2002	E. J. Henderson (LB)	Maryland

Maxwell Award
(College Football Player of the Year)

Year	Player	School
1941	Bill Dudley (HB)	Virginia
1984	Doug Flutie (QB)	Boston College
1986	Vinny Testaverde (QB)	Miami
1992	Gino Torretta (QB)	Miami
1993	Charlie Ward (QB)	Florida State
2001	Ken Dorsey (QB)	Miami

Davey O'Brien National Quarterback Award
(College Quarterback of the Year)

Year	Player	School
1984	Doug Flutie	Boston College
1986	Vinny Testaverde	Miami
1992	Gino Torretta	Miami
1993	Charlie Ward	Florida State
1999	Joe Hamilton	Georgia Tech
2000	Chris Weinke	Florida State

Thorpe Award
(College Defensive Back of the Year)

Year	Player	School
1987	Bennie Blades	Miami
1988	Deion Sanders	Florida State
1991	Terrell Buckley	Florida State

Florida wide receiver Dallas Baker leaps high in the air to score the game-winning touchdown against Florida State. The Gators were the 2006 national champions.

top of their game and the leaders of their respective conferences. It's the best of the ACC versus the best of the SEC. They've gone against each other ranked as number one and number two in the country. They've met in two Sugar Bowls. The Florida State Seminoles (ACC) beat the University of Florida Gators (SEC) in the 1995 Sugar Bowl. The Gators upset the Seminoles in the 1997 Sugar Bowl to win the national championship. The Florida Gators have thirty victories to lead the series rivalry.

Mascots and Nicknames

Mascots are a lot more than oversized, furry heads with permanently goofy facial expressions. They represent a piece of a university's history and are the most visible manifestation of school pride. They are the living symbols of a team nickname. The Atlantic Coast Conference (ACC) has many colorful and interesting characters that ignite school spirit.

Boston College Eagles

A Jesuit priest and Boston College alumnus, Reverend Edward J. McLaughlin, persuaded the school to choose an eagle as its mascot in 1920, believing it would represent majesty, power, and freedom. He envisioned an eagle swooping down to grab the "trophy of victory." Over the years, Boston College has used real and stuffed eagles to represent the school and its athletic teams. For the last forty years, however, they've been using a student in an eagle costume.

Clemson Tigers

This South Carolina university adopted the tiger as its mascot even before the days of John Heisman, the legendary football player and Clemson and Georgia Tech coach for whom the Heisman Trophy was named in 1935. The Tiger tradition often has been attributed to Walter Riggs, who coached Clemson in the late 1890s. Riggs previously had coached at Auburn University. The two schools

Known simply as "the Tiger," the Clemson mascot has been entertaining fans since 1954. The Tiger does push-ups after every Clemson touchdown.

share the same nickname. Clemson unveiled their current tiger paw logo in 1970. It was modeled after that of a real Bengal tiger.

Georgia Tech Yellow Jackets

The yellow jacket is a bee, but the term originally was used to describe clothing. It was a reference to the yellow-colored jackets that Georgia Tech fans wore to games in the early 1900s. The team eventually adopted the symbol of a fearsome-looking bee. Its bee is known as Buzz. Other nicknames used for Georgia Tech in the past were the Techs, Engineers, and Golden Tornadoes.

Maryland Terrapins

A terrapin is a large turtle that lives along the Atlantic coast. It is known for the diamond shapes on its shell. Adopting the terrapin as a mascot was the idea of a past University of Maryland president, H. C. Byrd. He proposed using the aquatic animal in 1932. The official terrapin of the school is named Testudo. A bronze statue of Testudo sits in the heart of the campus.

Miami Hurricanes and the Ibis

While the University of Miami's football team is referred to by the nickname the Hurricanes, the team mascot is different because there's really no way to animate a weather storm. So, the official mascot of the Hurricanes is a bird called the ibis. Ibises are wading birds with long legs and long, curved bills. According to tradition, the ibis is the last to hide before a hurricane and the first to reappear when it's over.

North Carolina Tar Heels and the Ram

The exact origins of the term "tar heel" are unknown. But most historians believe it relates to North Carolina's status as an important source of tar, pitch, and turpentine during the eighteenth and nineteenth centuries due to its abundance of pine trees. At some point in the nineteenth century, "tar heel" became an insulting term used to describe residents of North Carolina, who eventually came to embrace the expression with pride. A ram named Ramses became the University of North Carolina's official mascot in 1924. Jack Merritt was the inspiration for the ram. He was a ferocious Tar

Ramses, the beloved North Carolina mascot, makes an appearance on the field. Ramses has been the target of kidnapping attempts by students from conference rival Duke.

Heel football player who was known as the Battering Ram. A live ram has appeared at football games.

North Carolina State Wolfpack

In 1922, the students at North Carolina State turned an insult into a compliment. An angry fan complained to the school newspaper that the football team was acting like a "wolfpack." The criticism stuck and became a beloved nickname. The football team's logo is a struttin' wolf named Toughie. He wears a striped turtleneck emblazoned with the college's initials.

Mr. and Mrs. Wuf, as they are affectionately known, strut their stuff at every North Carolina State game.

Virginia Tech Hokies and the Fighting Gobbler

What's a Hokie? This nickname sprang from the imagination of O. M. Stull. Stull was a student at Virginia Tech in 1896 when he used the word in a school cheer he wrote and entered in a contest. Stull's cheer is still used today. It's called "Old Hokie." Some of the words are "Hoki, Hoki, Hoki, Hy. Techs, Techs, V.P.I." The Fighting Gobbler came along in 1912. Tech athletes had been called "Gobblers." This nickname produced a memorable mascot. The team used to bring live turkeys to football games until a student in a costume took over. Another name for the mascot is the Hokie Bird.

Duke Blue Devils

The Duke mascot is one of the most recognizable in all of college sports. It's known all over the country, since Duke often competes in nationally televised games, especially in basketball. The Blue Devil owes its identity to a famous French military squad in World War I. These soldiers earned a fierce reputation for their fighting skills in the French Alps. Their all-blue uniforms featured capes and berets. A Duke student newspaper began a campaign in 1922 to adopt the name, which most students didn't like. The newspaper continued to use the name anyway until it eventually gained wide-spread acceptance.

Florida State Seminoles

The students of Florida State voted in 1947 to select the Seminoles as the school's team name. Their original Seminole mascots did not look like real Seminole Indians. They looked like the kind of wild savage Indians typical of early cartoons and cowboy movies. This would change over time. Florida State has worked very hard to win the acceptance of the Seminole Nation. They got rid of the caricatured mascots and introduced two new ones, Chief Osceola and his horse, Renegade. The university also has expanded its awareness of Seminole history. Florida State received an official vote of support from the Seminole Tribal Council in 2005.

Virginia Cavaliers

Virginia has had many nicknames for its teams. Besides Cavaliers, the teams have been known as Wahoos, Hoos, V-men, Virginians, and Old Dominion. Cavaliers appeared as a team name after two students in 1923 wrote "The Cavalier Song" for a contest in the college newspaper. (A cavalier was an aristocratic horse-mounted soldier or knight who supported King Charles I of England during the

Chief Osceola and Renegade perform a dramatic spectacle before every Florida State home game. A student dressed in authentic Seminole attire rides around the stadium on an Appaloosa horse while brandishing a spear.

seventeenth century, the time of the founding of the Virginia Colony.) Wahoos is related to an old school cheer called "Wah-hoo-wah." Hoos is simply an abbreviation of Wahoos. The official mascot and logo of Virginia are associated with the Cavaliers. A person dressed in a Cavalier costume rides a horse during games. The logo is a "V" with two crossed sabers underneath it.

Wake Forest Demon Deacons

The football team from this small college in North Carolina used to be called the Baptists

The Demon Deacon rides in on his Harley-Davidson motorcycle before every Wake Forest home game.

in honor of their religious traditions. They remained the Baptists until 1923. A successful football season that year excited everyone on campus. Mayon Parker came up with the new name in his job as editor of the school newspaper. Parker used the name to describe their devilish play on the field and their fiery spirit. "Demon Deacons" was an instant hit. A mascot for the Demon Deacons was created in the early 1940s. A student showed up at a game dressed in a tuxedo and a top hat, the stereotypical outfit of a Baptist deacon. It was supposed to be a joke, but it quickly became part of the Wake Forest tradition.

GLOSSARY

Associated Press The largest and oldest news organization in the world.

Bowl Championship Series (BCS) Created in 1998 by the four biggest bowls (Orange, Sugar, Rose, and Fiesta) to determine a national college football champion.

bowl game A postseason college football game.

cavalier An armed horseman; a supporter of King Charles I during the English Civil War of the seventeenth century.

charter member A founder or original member of a group or organization.

conference A formal association or group.

deacon A church officer who assists the priest or minister.

defensive back A defensive player whose main responsibility is to cover wide receivers and defend against the pass.

down One of a series of four play attempts in which a team tries to advance the ball at least ten yards. If the offense gains ten yards within four downs, it receives another four downs and extends its opportunity to advance toward the opponent's end zone and score a touchdown or field goal.

draft A drawing by professional football teams to select new players from the college level.

exposure Frequent appearance before the public.

linebacker A defensive player positioned directly behind the line of scrimmage and the defensive linemen. His primary responsibility is to stop the run and defend against short passes.

line of scrimmage The line that separates the offensive and defensive linemen and upon which the football is placed before a play begins.

mascot Any person, animal, or thing chosen to represent a team.

media Radio, television, print, and Internet reporting; in this case, all the reporters and sportswriters who cover college football for various outlets.

mediocre Average or inferior skill level.

offensive coordinator The assistant coach in charge of helping plan and run the offense.

quarterback The offensive player who is in charge of advancing the ball to the goal by calling plays, orchestrating the offense, throwing passes, and handing the ball off to running backs.

rivalry A longstanding, emotionally charged competition between two teams.

sack To tackle a quarterback behind the line of scrimmage.

safety A defensive back farthest from the line of scrimmage; a safety provides defensive support to cornerbacks, the defensive backs who cover wide receivers.

syndication When rights to broadcast a program are sold to a number of television stations.

unique Something that is special and has no equal.

wide receiver An offensive player who catches forward passes from the quarterback.

FOR MORE INFORMATION

Atlantic Coast Conference
P.O. Drawer ACC
Greensboro, NC 27417-6724
(336) 854-8787
Web site: http://www.theacc.com

College Football Hall of Fame
111 South St. Joseph Street
South Bend, IN 46601
(800) 440-3263
Web site: http://www.collegefootball.org

National Collegiate Athletic Association (NCAA)
700 W. Washington Street
P.O. Box 6222
Indianapolis, IN 46206-6222
(317) 917-6222
Web site: http://www.ncaa.org

Web Sites

Due to the changing nature of Internet links, Rosen Publishing has developed an online list of Web sites related to the subject of this book. This site is updated regularly. Please use this link to access the list:

http://www.rosenlinks.com/icf/facc

FOR FURTHER READING

Barnhart, Tony. *Southern Fried Football: The History, Passion, and Glory*. Chicago, IL: Triumph Books, 2000.

Bradley, Michael. *Big Games: College Football's Greatest Rivalries*. Dulles, VA: Potomac Books, 2006.

Curtis, Brian. *Every Week a Season: A Journey Inside Big-Time College Football*. New York, NY: Ballantine Books, 2004.

DeCock, Luke. *Great Teams in College Football History*. Orlando, FL: Raintree, 2006.

Ellis, Steve. *Seminole Glory: A Look Back at Florida State's 1993 Championship Season*. Champaign, IL: Sports Publishing, 2003.

Ellis, Steve, and Bill Vilona. *Pure Gold: Bobby Bowden an Inside Look*. Champaign, IL: Sports Publishing, 2006.

Long, Gary. *Stadium Stories: Florida State Seminoles*. Guilford, CT: Globe Pequot, 2006.

MacCambridge, Michael. *ESPN College Football Encyclopedia: The Complete History of the Game*. New York, NY: ESPN Books, 2005.

Oslin, Reid. *Tales from the Boston College Sideline*. Champaign, IL: Sports Publishing, 2004.

Ours, Robert M. *Bowl Games: College Football's Greatest Tradition*. Yardley, PA: Westholme Publishing, 2004.

Pennington, Bill. *The Heisman: Great American Stories of the Men Who Won*. New York, NY: Regan Books, 2004.

Powell, K. Adam. *Border Wars: The First Fifty Years of Atlantic Coast Conference Football*. Lanham, MD: Scarecrow Press, 2004.

Quirk, James. *The Ultimate Guide to College Football: Rankings, Records, and Scores of the Major Teams and Conferences*. Champaign, IL: University of Illinois Press, 2004.

BIBLIOGRAPHY

"ACC, ABC, ESPN Reach $258 Million TV Deal." MSNBC.com. May 12, 2004. Retrieved January 10, 2007 (http://www.msnbc.msn.com/id/4962735).

"Boston College Agrees to Leave Big East for ACC." USAToday.com. October, 12, 2003. Retrieved January 10, 2007 (http://www.usatoday.com/sports/college/other/2003-10-12-bc-offer_x.htm).

Bowden, Bobby, and Steve Ellis. *Bobby Bowden's Tales from the Seminoles Sideline*. Champaign, IL: Sports Publishing, 2004.

Brown, Gerry, and Michael Morrison, eds. *2007 ESPN Sports Almanac*. New York, NY: ESPN Books, 2006.

Feldman, Bruce. *'Cane Mutiny: How the Miami Hurricanes Overturned the Football Establishment*. New York, NY: New American Library, 2005.

Fournier, Peter J. *The Handbook of Mascots and Nicknames*. Lithia, FL: Raja & Associates, 2004.

Sloan, Joanne, and Cheryl Watts. *College Nicknames and Other Interesting Sports Traditions*. Northport, AL: Vision Press, 1993.

Sumner, Jim. "Looking Back . . . The ACC's Beginnings with Bowl Games." TheACC.com. Retrieved January 6, 2007 (http://www.theacc.com/sports/m-footbl/spec-rel/010307aaa.html).

"Virginia Tech Sealing Move to ACC." USAToday.com. June 27, 2003. Retrieved January 10, 2007 (http://www.usatoday.com/sports/college/2003-06-27-acc-expansion_x.htm).

Whiteside, Kelly. "Hurricanes Announce Acceptance of ACC Invite." USAToday.com. June 30, 2003. Retrieved January 10, 2007 (http://www.usatoday.com/sports/college/2003-06-30-miami-acc_x.htm).

INDEX

About the Author

Jeremy Harrow lives in the heart of Seminole country in Fort Myers, Florida. He has a degree in media and communications. As a former community reporter, Jeremy has experience writing about national news from a local perspective. His first college football memory was watching quarterback Doug Flutie lead Boston College to victory in the 1985 Cotton Bowl.

Photo Credits

Cover (top and bottom), pp. 33, 35, 40 © Getty Images; pp. 1, 8, 17, 22, 27, 34 Shutterstock; pp. 4–5, 26, 31 Clemson University Athletic Department; p. 5 (logo) © AP Images; pp. 6, 28 College Football Hall of Fame; pp. 9, 10 Paul W. Bryant Museum/University of Alabama; pp. 11, 20, 24, 32 © www.istockphotos.com/Todd Bates; p. 13 Boston College; p. 18 © Collegiate Images/Getty Images; pp. 19, 23 © Icon SMI; pp. 21, 38 North Carolina State University Athletics; p. 25 Virginia Polytechnic Institute and State University; p. 37 Jeffrey Camarati; p. 41 Brian Westerholt/Sports On Film.

Designer: Tom Forget
Photo Researcher: Marty Levick